QUILT
STYLE

QUILT
STYLE

by Lucy A. Fazely

COURAGE
BOOKS
AN IMPRINT OF
RUNNING PRESS BOOK PUBLISHERS
Philadelphia • London

First published in the United States in 2002 by
Courage Books

Printed and bound in China

9 8 7 6 5 4 3 2
Digit on the right indicates the number of this printing

Library of Congress Cataloging-in-Publication
Number 2001094405

ISBN 0-7624-1273-9

First published in 2002 by
PRC Publishing Ltd,
64 Brewery Road, London N7 9NT
A member of the Chrysalis Group plc

This book may be ordered by mail from the publisher.
But try your bookstore first!

Published by Courage Books, an imprint of
Running Press Books Publishers
125 South Twenty-second Street
Philadelphia, Pennsylvania 19103-4399

Visit us on the web!
www.runningpress.com

Acknowledgments

The publisher wishes to thank all those who kindly supplied the photographs for this book.
Please see underneath captions for individual photo credits.

The photograph on the front cover shows "Rise & Shine, Inner City" by Martha W Ginn
(photo by Martha Ginn). The photograph on the back cover (top) shows "Yo-yo Quilt" by Mrs Rabitoy
(photo by Cheri Stearns). The photograph on the back cover (bottom left) shows "Reflections of Martha"
by Barbara Newman (photo by Barbara Newman). The photograph on the back cover (bottom right)
and on page 2 inside the book shows "Bristol Stars" by Judy Mathison (photo by Jack Mathison).

Contents

Introduction

Quilting has been an integral part of American history since the late 1700s. For over two centuries quilts have given women, and men, a forum to express their opinions and an outlet for their creativity. This handiwork has often been lost as the quilts were worn out by daily use for years on end, but those that have survived tell the story of their maker and their life. Some tales have been handed down through the generations and are clear, while others must be pieced together using the few clues found in the quilts themselves.

Most of the surviving examples have been passed down since the mid-1800s and later. Those remaining works from the earlier eras were probably the cream of the crop, the ones worthy of being set aside for special occasions. The majority of quilts were utilitarian and had to be replaced as the older ones wore out. With no less than three quilts on a bed, a woman with a large family had to use every spare moment and scrap to keep her family warm at night.

Quilting, although it can be an intricate art, is actually comprised of three very simple stitches.

Piecing is accomplished by a tight running stitch, whether by hand or machine, with a quarter inch seam allowance that is pressed to one side or the other. When piecing by hand, the stitches are anchored by taking a small backstitch or two at each end of the stitching line.

Appliqué, when done by hand, also employs a very simple stitch. Needle-turn appliqué, the most widely utilized technique, uses the point of the needle to turn under the seam allowance and then an invisible slip-stitch is taken around the edge of the piece. In this stitch, the thread is brought

Left: "Quilter at the Amand Broussard House." *A woman demonstrates quilting in a sitting room at the 19th century Amand Broussard House. The historic house stands at the Vermillionville Cajun/Creole fold village in Lafayette, Louisiana.* Photo circa 1997 by Dave G. Houser/ CORBIS.

up from the background fabric, a few threads on the bottom edge of the appliqué fold are caught by the needle, and then the thread is returned through the background fabric. A cotton or silk thread the same shade, or slightly darker, than the appliqué fabric is used. The more intricate the appliqué, the more skill it takes for the seamstress to achieve smooth curves and sharp points on her work.

The third use of stitches, and most visible, are the quilting stitches themselves. Several small knots are made at the end of a thread and then they are pulled between the layers of the quilt and anchored in the batting. The stitch used is just a simple running stitch. A rocking motion, with the needle going up and down through the layers is the goal, so the experienced quilter can take several stitches before pulling her needle through. With each stitch, a finger on the hand held under the quilt must be pricked to be sure that the stitch went through all the layers. Inexperienced quilters will have sore fingers for a while, until they build up a tough layer of skin on the surfaces most pricked. When the thread is at its end, it is once again knotted and anchored in the batting. For such a straightforward stitch, it is amazing what beauty can be obtained.

There has been so much love stitched into quilts over the centuries by women making them for their children, husbands, and friends. Is there any wonder why these pieces have been cherished and passed down through the generations for us to enjoy today?

Patchwork

BELOW:
"Antique Sunflower"
by an unknown maker.
Circa mid-1800s.
76 x 76 in.
Photo by House of White Birches.

Patchwork, the practice of sewing small pieces of fabric together to form a design, has an uncertain past. Each book or expert has their own opinion as to where the earliest examples can be found. The complete truth has been lost in our history, and we have only tidbits of information to base any theory on.

Patchwork is probably as old as sewing itself. The first recorded samples of patchwork may be in war banners carried onto the battlefield in Roman times. Perhaps, as some suggest, the history of patchwork could go back to when Adam and Eve first joined fig leaves to cover themselves. Whatever its humble start, throughout the centuries the use of patchwork has expanded to the point where it is currently used extensively in quilts, clothing, and other decorative forms.

The use of patchwork for quilted bedcovers is only a few hundred years old. In the 18th century patchwork was transformed when it was layered with a filling and lined with a backing fabric. These early quilts were made out of necessity, from any scrap of fabric that could be found, to keep their makers' families warm on cold winter nights. Since then, quilting has become the multi-million dollar industry it is today.

Patchwork designs are limited to mostly straight, and some curved, lines where the pieces are seamed together. Although this restricts the artisan, the variety of patchwork designs is seemingly limitless.

For centuries quilt makers have been cutting fabric into little pieces and sewing the pieces back together into quilt tops. In this chapter we will look at the designs that have been used for centuries, and some new innovative designs. By comparing the antique quilts with modern quilts we can see how much quilts have changed, while at the same time many of the earliest quilting traditions are continued today.

LEFT: "Antique Doll Quilt"
by Dorothy Wycoff, circa
1920. 13 x 23 in. Made in
Wyoming, Illinois, and
currently in the collection of
the maker's great, great niece
Sarah Kunc.
Photo by Cheri Stearns.

BELOW:
"Sunburst Medallion"
by unknown maker, circa
late 1800s. In the collection of
Sue Harvey, Lincoln, Maine.
Photo by House of White Birches.

One-patch Quilts

One-patch quilts are the simplest form of patchwork. Only one shape is used throughout. The color, value, and texture of the fabric patches form the design. Typically these quilts employ an all-over design such as diagonal rows of color (see right). A similar quilt with rows of color in a diamond shape around a central square is the "Trip Around the World."

"Postage Stamp" quilts, some of the most impressive one-patch quilts, are made entirely from tens of thousands of tiny pieces as small as three quarters of an inch square. How a woman must have needed to scrimp and save every bit of useable cloth to feel the need to piece so many diminutive pieces together.

The early doll quilt at the top of page nine uses squares pieced in an arrangement called "Boston Commons," a variation of "Trip Around the World." The fabrics were probably cut from salvageable parts of discarded clothing. As evidenced by the large uneven stitches, the quilt was most likely hand pieced and quilted by the maker when she was a child for her cherished doll. This quilt is very fragile now, after being used by four generations of women when they were children.

"Rise & Shine, Inner City" (below left) is an excellent example of just how elaborate a one-patch quilt can be. This modern quilt uses a

single shape, half a hexagon. The quilt maker spent years selecting fabrics purchased just for quilting, sewing together the pieces into "Y" sections and then bringing them all together to create the design she had envisioned in her head. The value of the fabrics used in each "Y" gives them the three-dimensional effect of buildings. She grouped the colors together, each color being a neighborhood, and then used carefully selected fabrics to blend the colors into each other. She describes it as, "...the sun shining in on the neighborhoods and waking up the city. The colors and even the quilting patterns of the neighborhoods are varied, but touching and joining to make the whole." The light section of the quilt is hand quilted with swirls extending from a center point depicting the sun. From there each "neighborhood" of color is hand quilted in with a different design.

According to Barbara Brackman's *Encyclopedia of Pieced Quilt Patterns*, one-patch quilts can also be made from right square triangles, equilateral triangles, rectangles, long strips, diamonds, hexagons, tumblers, kite shapes, parallelograms, pentagons, clamshell shapes, and an apple core shape, as well as many others.

Irish Chain

In use since at least the end of the 18th century, the "Irish Chain" block is an enduring pattern. Although it is not certain, it may have been named for the chain migration of the Irish to the United States. Immigration was often done by chain, where a family member who was already in the United States applied for a member still in the homeland. Since there was a limit on how many people a single citizen could sponsor, when the next group gained entry they, in turn, would sponsor another link in the chain. This is how so many of certain ethnic groups ended up in the same neighborhoods and cities. As a Certified Quilt Appraiser, Margaret Rouleau says, "Or did someone look at it (the quilt pattern) and say it looks like a chain and since you're Irish we should call it Irish Chain. In many cases I doubt that we will ever really know why or how a name was given and there is only speculation."

The "Irish Chain" quilt is usually single, double, or triple, determined by the number of squares that reach across the chain. The "Single Irish Chain" is a simple nine-patch block set with plain setting squares. A more unusual version is the "Multiple Irish Chain" (see right), also known as "Squares Around the World" or "Sunshine & Shadow," with five squares across on the chains. Jeanne Stauffer's husband's grandmother, Edna Stauffer, made this quilt. Jeanne writes, "I look at all the tiny squares, 3,025 of them, and wonder how long it took to piece them together by hand. Although I never met Edna, I share with her a love of quilting and treasure the memory I have of her through this beautifully hand pieced quilt. This quilt is among my most treasured possessions."

The "Double Irish Chain" quilt (left) was made as part of a class project by Nancy Manning, and is the first full-sized bed quilt Nancy ever made. In class, she was introduced to the modern aspects of quilting such as rotary cutting and machine piecing, while also learning the basics of stencils, pressing, and accuracy. Nancy says about this quilt, "It was made for my husband Gerald who wanted a heavy quilt like his Grandma used to make—well, I tried! The dear woman who quilted this for me agreed to quilt through two battings. ...It was not what my husband had in mind for a heavy quilt! ...He meant a scrap quilt made out of old suiting, coats, with a wool batting and flannel back."

Rail Fence

ABOVE (DETAIL) & RIGHT: "Slithering Snakes" by Susan Cleveland, West Concord, Minnesota, 1997. 62 x 83 in. Photo by S. Cleveland.

BELOW: "Allen's Hospital Quilt" by World War II volunteers in Battle Creek, Michigan, 1946. 45 x 47 in. In the collection of Allen and Ria Godfrey, Oscoda, Michigan. Photo by Cheri Stearns.

Between 1860 and 1930 in Wales and the northern counties of England a simple quilt of wide strips was popular. The "strippy," as it was known, was made of alternating bands of wool fabric stitched together and bordered by plain borders. The tops although simple, were the perfect showcase for elaborate quilting in challenging patterns such as flowers, spirals, medallions, and waves.

During wartime it was harder to get large pieces of new fabrics and quilters became frugal, cutting up and stitching together any scrap of fabric that was useable. However, scrap quilts have been around for a long time, popular not only during wars but in the early days of colonial America when England decreed that no cloth could be woven in the New World. Seamstresses who couldn't afford the high import tariffs on fabric from England, were forced to make do with what was on hand.

During World War II the Kellogg Sanitarium, in Battle Creek, Michigan, was taken over by the military and used as Percy Jones General Army Hospital. Allen Godfrey was a patient there for about six months of 1946, recovering from an infection he had picked up while serving in the Far East. Allen was given the simple wool quilt to the left, one of the many made by women's groups and given to injured World War II soldiers who had extended stays at the hospital.

"Rail Fence" quilts are a simple block with usually three to five rectangles lying side by side. When set together, alternating the rails by ninety degrees a zigzag pattern is formed across the quilt top. Just because a quilt is made with a simple block such as this doesn't mean it has to be boring as can be seen in the case of "Slithering Snakes" (right). Made by Susan Cleveland for her son, this fun quilt combines a traditional rail fence block with bright, modern fabrics and a fanciful original design.

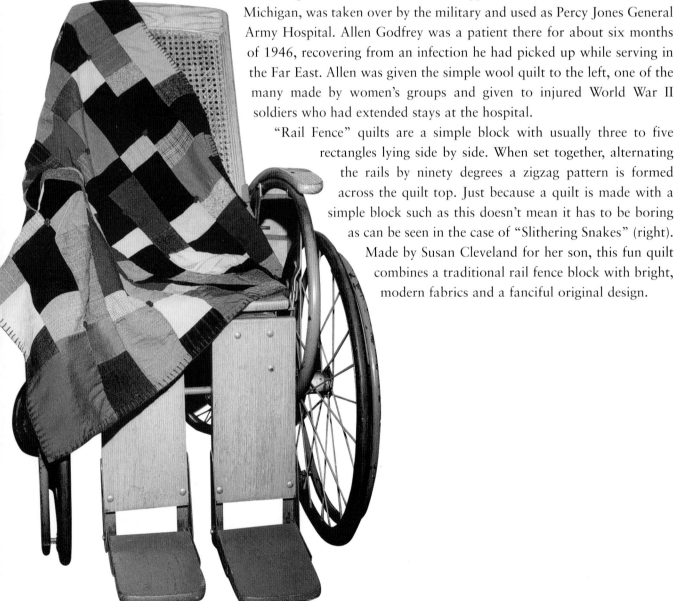

Grandmother's Flower Garden

Purchased from an antique festival in Cheboygan, Michigan in 1998, the late-19th century "Grandmother's Flower Garden" on this page has groupings of hexagons that form flowers. The pieces were pieced using a technique called English paper piecing. A piece of paper, without a seam allowance, is cut for each piece of the quilt. A piece of fabric is placed on the paper and its edges are finger pressed to the back. A running stitch is taken around the piece, holding the layers of fabric to the paper. The pieces are then slipstitched to each other. When finished the running stitch and papers are removed. The papers from this unfinished quilt, dating from 1884 to 1887, are cut from "all sorts of things like letters, hymns, etc." These are fascinating in their own right, providing as they do an insight into the maker's life. In this quilt they include:

Sampler-type handwriting, all upper case alphabet,
followed by lower case.
Detroit, Michigan, postmarks
Cleveland, Ohio, postmarks
An Orchard Lake, Michigan, postmark
"Dear Nellie"
A portion of an envelope addressed to "Nellie Nes..."
"9. Song—'I'll take...'" from a hymnal
Two-cent postage stamp on part of an envelope
Hospital heading on a brochure
"Hospital Private Room—$1.50" from a bill
Grand Opening announcement
"A. T. Brewer, Atty. at Law, 121 Superior St."
Portion of letterhead, "Vice President... ynolds"
"USA Treasurer...Farrand Training School"
Piece of paper listing "Vespers" and some women's names

Just as full of history is the modern quilt on this page, called "There Are No Snakes In My Garden." It was made by Barbara Newman for her daughter, Debbie. Debbie wanted a quilt with very small pieces and chose the "Grandmother's Flower Garden" design. On each "flower" the outside ring of petals are made up of twelve identical motifs. No two flowers are identical, with cows, butterflies, geese, flowers, rocking horses, and dinosaurs among the novelty prints used.

The original border design is a garden path appliquéd with memories of Barbara's life. Barbara explains the quilt's name, "My thoughts were also with my mother, who died several years ago. I remembered her saying over and over again 'Don't look for snakes! There are no snakes in my garden! If you really look, you will see all God's beauty, in both flowers and animals tucked away.' So my original garden became my mother's garden with many wonderful memories. I spent three years on this quilt."

Hexagon patterns can also be achieved by piecing each hexagon from three diamonds. This design is frequently seen in baby quilts, since it looks like a three-dimensional building block that small children play with.

ABOVE & BELOW (DETAIL): "There Are No Snakes In My Garden" *by Barbara Newman, Brandon, Mississippi, 1996. 88 x 104 in. This quilt is the winner of many awards including the prestigious Robert S. Cohan Master Award for Traditional Artistry, at the International Quilt Show in Houston, Texas, 1996.*

Both photos by B. Newman.

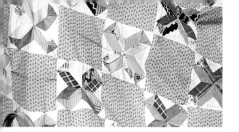

Four-patch

Early quilts used pieced or appliquéd designs to form an all-over design or a single large medallion center surrounded by borders. In the second quarter of the 19th century, quilt design shifted dramatically to multiple smaller blocks pieced into a whole top. These blocks were combined to form a top with strong vertical, horizontal, and, sometimes, diagonal lines. These smaller units were easier to work with and were portable so the busy seamstress could take part of a project with her when she was to be away from home for short or extended periods of time.

The four-patch block at its simplest is four equal size squares stitched together. These four-patch blocks can be stitched directly to each other, they can be joined with sashing strips between them, or with setting squares filling in every other block as can be seen in both quilts on this page.

The antique quilt below right uses a four-patch construction in which the original block is masked by the secondary design of stars and square-in-a-square blocks. If you look closely at the bottom left corner of the quilt you can see the original four-patch block. The upper right and lower left squares each have a large gold triangle and a smaller blue triangle in them. The two opposing squares each have two small red triangles.

Set in a four-patch block are "Drunkard's Path" squares in the bright and wild "Festivity" quilt (above right). The "Drunkard's Path" block, with one curved patch corner, was so named during the Temperance movement. At a time when women had little say in political matters and no vote, they were able to express their opinions and affiliation to groups in the quilt designs they chose to use. In the late 1800s, blue and white fabrics were often used to piece these quilts, signifying the colors of the Temperance movement.

Left: "Festivity"
by Christine Carlson,
Alpharetta, Georgia, 2000.
11½ x 11½ in.
Photo by House of White Birches.

Left: "Ramblin' Rose" *by an*
unknown maker, circa 1885.
57 x 81 in. In the collection of
Sue Harvey, Lincoln, Maine.
Photo by House of White Birches.

Nine-patch

Simple nine-patch blocks are similar to four-patch, except there are nine equal squares. Nine-patches can come in an almost unlimited number of varieties as the size of the central block changes in relation to the outer patches, usually becoming half or double the size of the outside corner squares. Each square can then be subdivided into smaller units, such as a four-patch, a nine-patch, half-square triangles (two triangles together forming a square) or quarter-square triangles (four triangles together forming a square). The varieties are almost limitless, with more being designed by modern quilters all the time.

Some of the commonly seen nine-patch blocks in this book are the "Feathered Star," "Variable Star," and "Lover's Knot."

In its simplest form, a nine-patch quilt can be striking in just two colors with a simple border. In the early sample at the top of this page the blocks are set on point, turned 90 degrees, forming the vertical and horizontal chains of squares across the quilt center. This quilt was made for Janet (Wood) Chappel by her great-grandmother, Fannie Mitchell, when she was born and is now in her daughter's collection.

The unusual setting for nine-patch blocks at the top of the page to the right has six blocks sewn around a muslin hexagon, with triangles of muslin filling in the outside edge of the circle, and between the circles. Janet Jones Worley made "Flames of Autumn" (left) because, in her own words, "The leaves of autumn each year always inspire me to make a quilt using those vibrant colors." The stars are a nine-patch with a large center square. The whole block is also a nine-patch with a large center square (the star) with "Flying Geese" triangles and plain setting squares filling out the block.

"'Chocolate Chips' (below right) was designed during the time I was working on my book *Quilts for Chocolate Lovers*. Sometimes quilts are born first on paper and others are inspired by fabric, but this quilt came about because of a warm and delicious chocolate chip cookie freshly baked in my oven!" says Janet. This quilt is a combination of two nine-patch blocks, the "Variable Star" and a nine-patch with four-patches in the corner squares.

The nine-patch stars in these last two quilts were often used in album quilts. These quilts were made by groups of women to commemorate a special event, raise money for a charitable cause, or to honor someone special. The center square of the star, or other block, was left unpieced and was made of a light colored material, if not muslin. In the center of each block a different person would sign their name.

LEFT: "Rainbow of Rings"
by unknown maker, circa
1930s. 70 x 90 in.
In the collection of Carol
Scherer, Moline, Illinois.
Photo by House of White Birches.

LEFT: "Chocolate Chips"
by Janet Jones Worley,
Huntsville, Alabama, 2000.
45 x 54 in.
Photo by House of White Birches.

Log Cabin

ABOVE: "Antique Log Cabin" *by Emma Bratt, Detroit, Michigan, circa 1898. 69 x 47 in. From the collection of Allen & Ria Godfrey, Oscoda, Michigan.* Photo by Cheri Stearns.

BELOW: "Antique Log Cabin" *by the sisters of William McAllister, 1878. Currently in the collection of his great-granddaughter, Cindi Van Hurk, Lincoln, Michigan. 66 x 80 in. The blocks are laid out in* Sunshine and Shadow *design.* Photo by Cheri Stearns.

Often when someone hears about log cabin quilts, they visualize a representational rendition of a log cabin. Actually, a log cabin block is based on a center square with "logs" around it. The center square is often red, representing the flames burning in the hearth of the home.

There are many different configurations of the "Log Cabin" block as shown on the next few pages. The differences in the blocks are achieved by the placement of light and dark valued fabrics and the order in which the logs are added to the block.

The antique "Log Cabin" quilt below was made in 1878 for William McAllister by his six sisters in Hensall, Ontario, Canada. The sisters were dressmakers and milliners and it is believed that many of the fabrics were from their scrap baskets.

Some of the materials in the quilt, are known to be woven by William's grandfather, the first William McAllister, who came to Canada from Glasgow, Scotland. He was a weaver by trade.

Before his marriage, the younger William was building his homestead and working on the Canadian Pacific Railroad near Winnipeg, Manitoba. He slept in his wagon, kept warm by this quilt.

When William and his family came to Michigan around 1890, the quilt was part of their household that came with them. Today this fragile heirloom remains in the possession of his descendants.

The early quilt at the top of the left hand page is in poor shape, with holes and frayed edges from many years of neglect. The quilt was kept in the attic of Clarence and Marion Godfrey's Florida home for 20 years. When their son, Allen Godfrey, was cleaning out the attic he found a nasty box wrapped in old carpeting. His wife, Ria, told him to just throw out the whole mess. Not one to throw things away, he looked in the box and found four quilts, including this log cabin made of one inch strips pieced on a foundation and set in a sunshine and shadow design. Allen tells that his great grandmother, Emma Bratt, quilted up until her death in 1917. His mother used to have to thread her grandmother's quilting needles each morning before going to elementary school, since Emma's eyes were too bad to do it herself.

In the modern version above, 45 colored prints were used and placed in order of their placement on the color wheel. The fabrics were then separated into five piles of nine fabrics. The blocks were made so the middle of the nine fabrics for each block was the center square of the block. The logs were added to the sides, keeping the same color placement. The blocks were laid in a "Straight Furrows" configuration, named for rows of plowed earth.

Courthouse Steps

ABOVE AND BELOW:
"Antique Courthouse Steps"
by unknown maker, circa
1880s–90s. 72 x 72 in.
This quilt is in the collection
of Sandra L. Hatch, Lincoln,
Maine.
Photo by House of White Birches.

The "Log Cabin" block, dating back as far as the late 1700s, reached its height of popularity in the mid-19th century and traditionally starts with a central square and then the logs are added in a circular manner around the block. "Courthouse Steps," a variation on the theme, starts with a central square and then logs are added to two opposing sides, then the other two opposing sides, alternating with each addition.

The old example seen here is made with many conversational prints, which were popular in the late 1800s. The red or black designs such as animals, fireworks, sewing implements, and other recognizable objects were printed on white shirting-weight fabric.

Fabrics often help when dating a quilt since there is decent documentation on the types of weaving, style of prints, design motifs, dyes used, and printing methods used throughout history. Quilts are assumed to be from a certain period if the fabrics and quilt design match up to that period. For instance, indigo blue prints were from the 1840s, rust colored browns and Centennial motifs were from the 1870s, shirting materials in dark gray and black were from the 1900s, and then in the 1920s soft pastels and floral prints were popular.

Dating modern quilts will be much more difficult since so many quilters are using vintage fabrics and many reproduction fabric lines are available. Hopefully these quilts will have the date and maker's name inscribed on the quilt, making the job of future quilt historians easier.

Pineapple

The variations that can be achieved altering the "Log Cabin" block are almost limitless. The antique quilt below, made from silk, woven wools, and wool challis hand pieced on a foundation, uses a hexagon in the center instead of a square. Logs are then added to six sides, with the black logs added to two opposite sides creating the black diamond shapes.

The "Pineapple" quilt, a similar variation, uses a square in the center with four logs on each side. The corners are trimmed at 45 degree angles and then four diagonal logs are added to the corners. In this configuration the side logs vary in value from the diagonal logs, creating a series of light and dark pineapple looking shapes across the quilt top.

Over 50 hand-dyed solid colored fabrics were used to make the beautiful variation to the right. The blocks were constructed by machine using a paper foundation, which was removed before the quilt was sandwiched. The center of each block is a rectangle comprised of two triangles. Each log is then stitched on, moving in a counter-clockwise direction. Careful planning was needed to place the colors and values in this quilt and make it as spectacular as it is. The triangular shape of the logs is what gives the blocks a twist, giving much movement to this piece.

Typically "Log Cabin" quilts were bulky. There were many seams in the top, the layer of foundation they were sewn on, and a batting and backing—all combining to make it difficult to hand quilt.

ABOVE: "Log Cabin Twist" *by Lynn Graves, Chama, New Mexico, 1995. 30 x 30 in.* Photo by House of White Birches.

LEFT: "Hexagonal Comfort" *by Marie Howard, circa 1860–1880. 67½ x 80 in. In the collection of Xenia Cord, Kokomo, Indiana.* Photo by House of White Birches.

Star

Star quilt patterns have always been popular in American quilt making, stars with four, six, and eight points being the most used. An eight-pointed star pieced from eight large diamonds, each made up of smaller diamonds is an enduring symbol of our history. The names given to these quilts often signify the religious beliefs of colonial Americans and can be traced to the bible. Other names have come from the state names created as the territories joined the Union, and still others from famous people. In 1718 the Lemoyne brothers were honored with a block named the "Lemoyne Star" after they founded of the City of New Orleans.

The quilt below is an example of "Texas Star," and was pieced entirely from hand-dyed fabrics at the end of the 18th century. Its maker, known only as Grandma Johnson, lived from 1860 until 1960. She was said to have won a Golden Thimble Award for her quilting. The quilt was donated to the local historical museum when her grandson's widow moved away, wanting it to stay near her late husband's family home.

This beautiful antique "Lone Star" quilt (right) was rescued from the trunk of a car where it was being used as a liner. A very popular design, according to Barbara Brackman's *Encyclopedia of Pieced Quilt Patterns* it has taken on many names over the years including "Star of the East," "Star of Bethlehem," "Blazing Star," "Rising Star," "Pride of Texas," "Star of Stars," and "Rising Sun" among others.

The American Indians in the Northern Plains were taught the art of quilt making by early American settlers. They use this same design, calling it the *Morning Star*, symbolizing the start of a new day. They often incorporate a bald eagle or other motif built from the diamonds of the star.

Based on the traditional "Lone Star" block, "Party of Three" at the top of this page is anything but traditional with its bright hand-dyed fabrics, generous use of thick decorative threads, piping, and prairie points. The offset backgrounds give it a bit of asymmetry leaving the viewer with a feeling of being at a lively party with lots of noise, people, and fun. No wonder this quilt has won three coveted quilt awards and quilter/designer Susan Cleveland is sought out to teach and lecture nationally.

Feathered Star

ABOVE (DETAIL) & BELOW:
"Feathered Star" by Evaline McKay Forman, Mize, Smith County, Mississippi, circa 1899. 61 x 80 in. Hand quilted in an overall clamshell pattern. In the collection of Loney Ward, Jackson, Mississippi.
Photo by B. Newman.

Quilts haven't always been treasured family heirlooms and were often discarded after the death of the quilt maker. The interesting "Feathered Star" on this page was picked out of the trash by Desmond Holmes Ward, a grandson of the maker, Evaline McKay Forman, when they were settling the estate. The quilt is now in the collection of Loney Ward, Desmond's widow. Why did Evaline make nine blocks with tan points, two blocks with red points, and one with tan and red points? Did she run out of fabric, or was she trying to symbolize something? Unfortunately, the answers died with her.

The modern rendition of the "Feathered Star" pattern at the bottom of the page to the right was made with fabrics using the same traditional coloring of the antique example.

The "Feathered Star" derives it name from the intricately pieced triangles that grace the edges of the star. Many of the older quilts have

LEFT: "Pretty Flaky" *by Susan Cleveland, West Concord, Minnesota, 1999. 41 x 41 in. This modern Feathered Star quilt was made using a "discharge" technique, bleaching out the light blue fabric leaving the snowflake designs.*
Photo by S. Cleveland.

BELOW: "Feathered Star Wall Hanging" *by Cynthia Van Hurk, Lawton, Oklahoma, 1986. 47 x 47 in. Machine pieced and hand quilted.*
Photo by Cheri Stearns.

triangles that are different sizes from the inside corners of the star point. Piecing was a tricky matter as the triangles were often made to fit, but modern quilters have some advantages in using speed techniques to get accurate results. Even so, it is not an easy design to master.

Like a cold Minnesota day, "Pretty Flaky" (above) literally sparkles from hundreds of small glass beads held in place on its surface with quilting stitches. This design started with a traditional "Feathered Star" and hand-dyed fabrics. Combined with a leafy background print, foundation pieced icicles, and snowflake blocks it is absolutely stunning. Although the white snowflakes appear to be appliquéd they are actually a "discharge" design, created when the design is bleached out of the colored background fabric. When quilted, the snowflakes were slightly stuffed, giving them a three dimensional effect. The icicles also started out as the same light blue fabric as the snowflake blocks, but were sprayed with a bleach solution leaving them dappled looking. The outside edge consists of two rows of piping with small beads sewn between them.

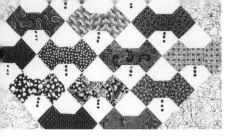

Bow Tie

Dating as far back as the late 1800s, the "Bow Tie" quilt block can be made a couple of different ways. It can be made as a four-patch, with triangles added to the inside corners of the background squares, making the knot in the center, or, as in the antique "Bow Tie" below and the modern "Formal Bow Tie" above, a three-dimensional square "knot" can be stitched to the center of a four-patch block. Barbara MacDonald used black and white fabrics left over from another project and wanted it to look more formal, so she hand quilted narrow lines simulating a pin-tucked tuxedo shirt then added shank buttons to complete the look.

According to Barbara Brackman's *Encyclopedia of Pieced Quilt Patterns*, different names have been given to this block and its variations throughout the years, including "Necktie," "Magic Circle," "True Lover's Knot," and "Dumbbell Block."

Each time a quilt is made, the maker either keeps the name she knows it as or renames it according to something of importance in her life. Women who had little voice in their era's political events showed their approval or disapproval of events by naming quilt blocks with names such as: "White House Steps," "Slave Chain," "Democratic Rose," and "Whig's Defeat."

Those crossing North America in colonial times suffered hardship and loss, and consequently gave their quilt block descriptive names such as "Crosses & Losses," "Winding Trail," and "Rocky Road to Kansas."

Love and marriage were never far from a young girls' mind as she stitched quilts for her dowry, giving us romantic names like "Young Man's Fancy," "Lover's Knot," and "Wedding Ring."

A strong belief in God and trust in the Bible spurred the names of blocks like "Jacob's Ladder," "Walls of Jericho," "Solomon's Puzzle," and "Star of Bethlehem."

Double Wedding Ring

The "Double Wedding Ring" quilt has to be an all-time favorite of quilters, although many are intimidated by its complexity and curved edges. Even though most variations seem almost identical, there are some major differences in construction and design that aren't always obvious to the untrained eye. The number of wedges in each arc is sometimes an indication of how old the quilt is, with modern quilts frequently using fewer wedges than their antique counterparts. Some employ a single large square where the wedges meet, while others use two colored squares that form a four-patch when the blocks are pieced together. Some versions don't use an arc of pieced wedges, but an arc cut from a single piece of print cloth. Yet another version divides the central background diamond into four pieces so the blocks can be pieced in square units so no long curved seams need to be sewn. This version is well suited for the modern quilter and machine piecing. When the wedges in the arcs are replaced by triangles instead of wedges, the pattern becomes the "Pickle Dish" or "Indian Wedding Ring."

Most versions are pieced into circles and then the rings combined by the setting diamonds. Different patterns call for different techniques, and most are not easy to execute well unless hand stitched by an experienced seamstress.

"Opposites Complement" (below) is a modern interpretation of the traditional "Double Wedding Ring" design, with the rings broken apart and appliquéd on a large print floral fabric. Made as a 40th anniversary gift for her parents, the quilt signifies how they are "opposites yet complement each other nicely." Her selection of red/pink and green hand-dyed fabrics are opposites on the color wheel, adding to the quilts' symbolism.

ABOVE: "Squashed Double Wedding Ring," *date and maker unknown.* 76½ x 86¼ *in. In the collection of Jodi Warner, South Jordan, Utah.* Photo by House of White Birches.

LEFT: "Opposites Complement" *by Susan Cleveland, West Concord, Minnesota. Approximate size 68 x 81 in. From the collection of Bob & Judy Lehms* Photo by S. Cleveland in Lehms home.

Circular

Circular quilt designs are dramatic to look at but can be challenging for the quilt maker. "Antique Sunflower Quilt" (below right) is an excellent example of a well-constructed circular block. These blocks are not easy to piece and still maintain flatness for the simple reason that there are so many pieces that need to come together and form a perfect circle. This design starts with a central circle of muslin, surrounded by a row of triangles, diamonds, and then another row of triangles. The finished design was probably then appliquéd to a whole square of muslin, with the muslin under the design later cut away to reduce bulk. The "Flying Geese" sashing on this unfinished top adds movement and makes it even more visually exciting.

Barbara Newman was a professional woman, who had worked as a banker for 45 years. She didn't have time to take up a hobby such as quilting when she agreed to accompany a friend to a meeting, and firmly stated that she would not learn to quilt. In the ten years since, she has made four bed size quilts and a number of smaller quilts, all meticulously hand pieced and quilted. Her quilts have won, and continue to win, prizes and recognition around the country and internationally. "Reflections of Martha" seen at the top and bottom left of this page was her first full-sized quilt and is a masterpiece of design and color. The center of the quilt is made up of "Baby Bunting" blocks, surrounded by an original appliquéd border. "Quilting," Barbara says, "fulfills my need to create, gives me a way to release stress, and keeps me from having to do housework."

Circular quilt patterns proliferated from the late 1800s right through to the first half of the 20th century. It is almost as if each quilt maker took it upon themselves to better their neighbor by using a more difficult block with more pieces, requiring increased skill with the needle. The example to the right, "Sunshine Aster," is like most circular blocks in that the design was probably hand pieced and then appliquéd to a foundation. This block is very similar to a "Dresden Plate" (see Chapter Two) except that half the rays are muslin, where in a "Dresden Plate" all the rays are colored prints and have a rounded end.

"Sunburst Medallion" (see page 9) is comprised of a dizzying array of diamonds and triangles. Perhaps these intricate designs were saved for the quilting bee frame, where all the maker's friends and family could see what a talented craftsperson she was, saving the simpler quilts for the frame at home.

Quilting bees, named after the busy homemaker, were a much anticipated gathering of women who worked together to quilt a special piece, such as a bridal quilt—only the best quilters were invited to a bee. The quilt to be finished would be stretched taut on a large frame. Marking the design would be done with thimbles, teacups, and plates as templates. Quilters would work on it from every angle while sharing chitchat and gossip. When the quilting was done as far as could be reached, the quilt was rolled giving the women access to the inner sections. With so many experienced seamstresses working, the quilt would be completely finished by the end of the day.

Quilting bees were such large events that the hostess was not expected to actually sit and do any quilting. She was much too busy seeing to her guests' needs and preparing a large meal that they would all share when the men came home from the fields. Young women, who had not become proficient with the needle, were given kitchen duties and would try to improve their skills so they would be invited to sit at the frame the next year. The evening would be filled with song as they held a square dance and took a break from their seemingly endless duties. These events were greatly anticipated through the long, cold winters and an invitation to one was always welcome.

Although quilting bees are not the social center of any woman's life anymore, women, and men, still gather for quilt guild meetings, classes, lectures, shows, and the occasional old-fashioned quilting bee. It is through these events that they have a chance to share their thoughts and talents with others, much the same as their predecessors did.

ABOVE: "Sunshine Aster," maker and date unknown. 82 x 82 in. In the collection of Carol Scherer, Moline, Illinois. Photo by House of White Birches.

Crazy

"Crazy Quilts," or "crazies" as some call them, were most popular in the Victorian Era, during the second half of the 19th century, though they date back to colonial times. With no actual block design, scraps of cotton, satin, velvet, silk, or wool were randomly stitched onto a foundation fabric. Edges were usually covered by embroidery stitches, frequently a feather, herringbone, or other decorative stitch. Crazies were a blank canvas for women to showcase their embroidery skills and the patches sometimes have decorative stitches on them, commemorating something special to the seamstress. A common theme in the embroidery was oriental motifs because of the opening up of trade between Japan and the United States and the subsequent interest in the area. Certain flowers were used because they had meaning; the rose for love, the lily for purity, and forget-me-nots for remembrance. It is not hard to imagine how working on one of these quilts during a bleak winter might have cheered a work weary wife.

The backs of crazy quilts were usually covered by a lining to hide the backs of the stitches and the seams. The two layers were tacked together, and the edges turned in and slip-stitched together.

"Crazy Star" at the top of the page is a fragile textile on the verge of being lost. Although it was never bound and used, the satins have shattered and deteriorated. Made up of nine blocks it is set with sashing and interesting pieces of cloth in the cornerstones, which are stamped with flags, flowers, and names of places. The stamps include the names; Dutch East Indies, Munich, Modena, and Australia. Did the maker, or someone she knew, travel to these places? Was this quilt made to commemorate the travels of a sailor in service to his country?

"Crazy Quilt" to the left was typical of the 1930s, using a folded technique to create the 25 blocks. The gold fringe was sewn down by machine and a hand-sewn herringbone stitch was used over the seams. This quilt was donated to the local historical museum when the Alpena Garment Company (1866–1985) went out of business. The quilt had been used to grace their office walls for many years.

"Crazy-Patch Star," on the right, is visually stunning with the strong contrast between the red, cream, and brown crazy patch diamonds.

Medallion Quilts

ABOVE: "The Garden Court Compass" *by M'Liss Rae Hawley, Freeland, Washington, 1997. 63 x 78 in.* Photo by Michael A. Hawley.

BELOW: "Cherries Jubilee Celebration" *by Barbara Newman, Brandon, Mississippi, 1998. 48½ x 48½ in.* Photo by B. Newman.

Some quilts are made to symbolize what is important in the maker's life. "The Garden Court Compass" (above) was made by M'Liss Rae Hawley as a celebration of their home on beautiful Whidbey Island, located in Puget Sound north of Seattle, Washington. The "Mariner's Compass" medallion was constructed on a paper foundation, with a chrysanthemum print from an antique kimono gracing the center, in honor of the many Japanese exchange students they have hosted over the years. She describes the rest of the quilt, "the compass is surrounded by; flying geese, a forest of many trees with stars above. The Coast Guard and lighthouse have a fence, garden, and dachshunds in the beach grass. The Coast Guard house has a dog and cat in the windows and a potted flower on the porch. The Bargello border is a beautiful interplay of light and dark values, combining many of the fabrics in the quilt. This coastal composition will leave admirers smelling salt air and hearing the sea gulls cry."

Medallion quilts are usually very striking with a large center design surrounded by borders. "Cherries Jubilee Celebration" (below left) definitely falls into that category. Barbara made this quilt as part of the "Pieces of the Past Challenge" in 1998 sponsored by Better Homes & Garden's *American Patchwork & Quilting* magazine. Quilters were given ten antique blocks to choose from but they only had to use one. Barbara chose to use the "Seven Sisters" and "Cherries" blocks. Barbara explains her choices, "Our bank had just been sold. The purchasing bank's logo was a six-pointed star while my bank's logo was very similar to the cherries block. My quilt shows how the purchasing bank came in, jumped in the middle, spread us apart and surrounded us while the trapunto cherry design shows our bank fading away." The quilt was completely hand pieced, appliquéd and quilted. Barbara's hard work paid off with a second place win that was soon followed by other awards and honors.

Mariner's Compass

A "Mariner's Compass" is a difficult design to execute with its long thin triangles radiating from the center. Traditionally pieces are hand pieced due to the exacting nature of the work. These blocks can have as few as 12 points and as many as 185. With the advent of new technologies this kind of design is easier to accomplish, but no less dramatic.

A modern interpretation of the "Mariner's Compass" design, "Twirling Tassels" (below) is made with bright hand-dyed fabrics. Traditionally a hand pieced design, this quilt was actually machine pieced and machine appliquéd with both machine and hand quilting. The designer had fun embellishing the quilt with piping in the border and binding, hundreds of small red prairie points, vintage beads, and thread work. It all comes together to make it a really spectacular quilt.

BELOW: "Twirling Tassels" by Susan Cleveland, West Concord, Minnesota, 2001. 54 x 62 in. Quilt shown on Americana Carousel in Camp Snoopy, Mall of America, Bloomington, Minnesota. Photo by S. Cleveland.

Floor Designs

Although there is much debate in the traditional art world as to whether a quilt is art, quilters know that a masterpiece is a masterpiece whether it was painted, sculpted, or stitched. And "Bristol Stars" on the right is a masterpiece of design and workmanship that was inspired by a marble floor in Bristol Cathedral in England. With the help of her husband, Judy adapted the design using Claris Draw software on a Macintosh computer and printed the patterns onto paper. She was able to machine stitch the entire top using a freezer paper method of foundation piecing. The quilt was finished with hand and machine quilting. This spectacular quilt has graced the cover and pages of books, magazines, and calendars and won the prestigious Master Award at the International Quilt Festival in Houston, Texas in 1999.

Another quilt inspired by a floor is "With A Little Help From My Friends" (left). Ami Simms took the design from an ancient Roman floor in a place called Ostia Antica, just outside of Rome, Italy. She was, as she puts it, "collecting floors that could be interpreted in cloth for my fourth book, *Classic Quilts: Patchwork Designs From Ancient Rome.*"

Although she was able to give correct instruction in the book, she encountered problems while hand stitching the border while on a teaching trip in Australia. It wasn't until she returned home that she realized why her border was not working the way it should. "Faced with a looming deadline, I did the next best thing. I asked my friend, Maggie DuPuis, who can piece *anything* on a machine what to do and she showed me how to almost invisibly appliqué a new border in place by machine—and just in time. I finished the quilt, made the deadline, and 'With A Little Help From My Friends' now lives on the front cover." Speaking of the first border she adds, "The magnificent hand appliquéd border lives on the back of the quilt!"

T-blocks and House Blocks

ABOVE: "Crossed T's" *by Christine Carlson, Alpharetta, Georgia, 1999. 17¼ x 17¼ in.* Photo by House of White Birches.

BELOW: "Double T," *unknown maker. circa 1930s. 57 x 88 in. In the collection of Jayne Gault, Etna Green, Indiana.* Photo by Sue Kruger.

The Temperance Movement in the United States addressed a social issue that women were particularly interested in since they were often the ones with a problem when their men drank. Without financial means to support themselves, they had no choice but to stay with a drunken spouse. Women were involved in the Temperance Movement from the early 1800s and were a significant force by the 1870s. In an era when women had no vote and no real voice in changing the world around them, they used any method that they could in order to be heard. One small way a woman could express her support of the cause was in the blocks she chose to use in her quilts.

Although made in the 1930s "Double-T" (below left) is an example of a "T" block commonly used to show support for the Temperance Movement. It is a summer spread that was purchased at an estate sale for $50.00. It was machine pieced and lightly quilted, with no batting.

According to Barbara Brackman's *Encyclopedia of Pieced Quilt Patterns* some other names for such blocks were: "Capital T," "The T Quilt," "T Blocks," "Four T's," "Cross of Temperance," and "Temperance Tree." "Crossed T's" (above) is a modern version of the basic block.

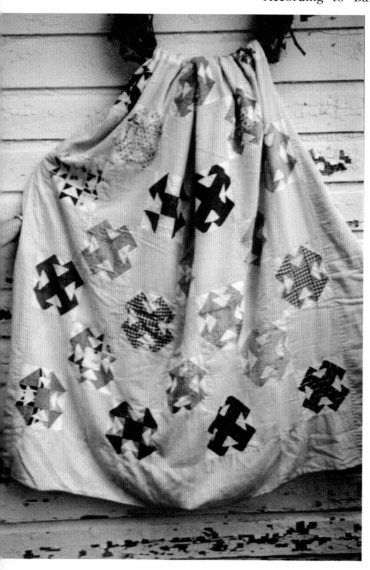

House blocks were a way for the homemaker to show her dedication to the home and family. "Little House in the Big Woods" (above right) was an innovative way for the maker to use a variety of house blocks in different sizes placing larger houses in the front to give the piece a sense of depth. The tree was strip pieced and appliquéd on the background. The moon and people were cut from print fabrics and then appliquéd in place. The background is machine quilted, with variegated threads, in meandering lines like paths through the woods.

Schoolhouse blocks gained popularity in the late 1800s. The "Strip Piecing" referred to in the name of the small modern quilt to the right is a technique of machine stitching strips together and then cutting them apart, rather than cutting smaller pieces and sewing them together individually. A rotary cutter is very handy for this. Similar to a pizza cutter, it has a sharp, circular razor blade for cutting up to eight layers of fabric at a time. When used with a special mat and acrylic rulers, cutting out a quilt can be done accurately and in a fraction of the time that it would take with scissors and templates.

ABOVE: "Little House in the Big Woods" *by Martha W. Ginn, Hattiesburg, Mississippi, 1997.*
47 x 40 in. From the collection of Mark & Melody Ginn. Photo by M. Ginn.

LEFT: "Schoolhouse for Strip-Piecing" *by Linda Denner, 1995.*
Photo by House of White Birches.

Tree of Life

Nature was a common theme in quilt designs, which is only fitting since the colonists and pioneers lived intimately with it in all its glory, as well as when it was at its most brutal. Mountains, flowers, and water, as well as other aspects of nature were well represented in quilts. The "Tree of Life" pattern seen in the photograph below was favored as a quilt design because of its beauty and its religious theme of eternal life.

There are a large number of variations on the "Tree of Life" design that are called "Pine Tree." (Since pine trees can be found everywhere in North America, it is not hard to see how the name came to signify so many varied configurations of the block.) The number of rows and columns of triangles that make up the branches are the most noticeable differences in the blocks, with the width and length of the trunk also varying.

"Pine Tree" (above) was purchased from an antique dealer for $50 in 1995. It was machine pieced and has lots of detailed hand quilting. The quilt was originally purchased as a cutter quilt by Jayne Gault. (A cutter quilt is a quilt that is worn beyond repair and is cut into small pieces to be used in smaller pieces such as decorative pins, pillows, toys, etc.) Jayne says that only the binding was worn, and she couldn't bring herself to cut it up.

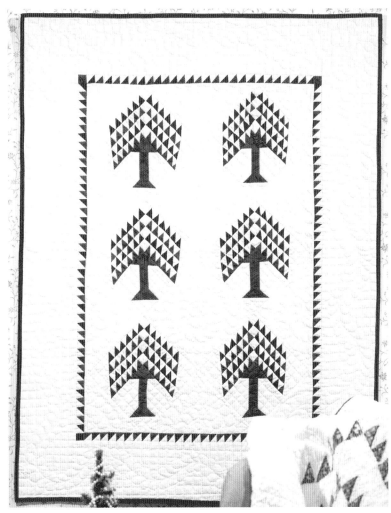

Another fine example of a "Pine Tree" quilt can be seen at the top of the page to the right. It was made in the 1930s using fabrics popular at the time, though they are unusual for a block of this type. The coloring in the modern "Spruce Tree Farm" to the right is more representational of the natural theme.

LEFT: "Pine Tree" *by an
unknown maker, circa 1930s.
62 x 77½ in. In the collection
of Mary Jo Kurten, Hot
Springs Village, Arizona.*
Photo by House of White Birches.

BELOW: "Spruce Tree Farm"
by an unknown maker, 1998.
Photo by House of White Birches.

Baskets

ABOVE: "Poinsettias" by Jill Reber, Granger, Iowa, 1998. 57¼ x 57¼ in. Photo by House of White Birches.

BELOW: "Fruit Baskets" by unknown maker, circa 1930s. 73¼ x 83⅝ in. In the collection of Sandra L. Hatch, Lincoln, Maine. Photo by House of White Birches.

BELOW RIGHT: "Anne's Basket" by Jill Reber, Granger, Iowa, 1997. Photo by House of White Birches.

Long a favorite with quilters, basket blocks bring to mind a stitcher's sewing basket, a basket full of posies or fresh baked bread. They are a symbol of good times in a simpler life. Barbara Brackman's *Encyclopedia of Pieced Quilt Patterns* identifies over 130 different pieced basket blocks, more than the number of identified tree blocks, house blocks, or flower blocks. Truly, quilters have a love affair with their baskets!

Although the two basket quilts below were created about 70 years apart, they are remarkably similar. They both use the identical block pattern set on point (turned 90 degrees) and have setting squares between the pieced blocks. It is likely that the older quilt was hand pieced and the newer quilt machine pieced.

A basket combined with flowers makes up "Poinsettias," above, a new wall quilt based on a variation of an old pattern, "The Carolina Lily." Definitely a seasonal quilt with its red and green coloration, this wall quilt would be a welcome addition to any home during the holidays.

Decorative wall quilts were rare in the days when all of a woman's energies were put to use just keeping up with the daily chores. Today's quilters, however, enjoy the option of working on smaller projects, without having to invest the time and money necessary to make a large bed quilt. A quilter is able to experiment with a larger variety of different blocks and fabric combinations by making projects like wall quilts, table runners, and banners. In a quilter's world, filled with new fabric lines every few months and new books of patterns constantly being published, there are more projects than he or she will ever have time to do in one lifetime. Small projects help them keep up, without being overwhelmed.

Colorwash

Colorwash is a modern technique that was started in England by a quilter named Deidre Amsden and made popular in the US by Pat Magaret and Donna Slusser with their book *Watercolor Quilts*. Two-inch squares of busy printed fabrics are pieced together to form a quilt top that resembles an Impressionist painting. The watercolor look is created with careful placement of the fabrics so there is a blending from one to the next creating a flow from light to dark. "Watercolor Crucifix" (right) started as a 50th wedding anniversary gift for a friend who wanted to donate a wall quilt to her church in honor of the occasion. "Ladybug's Flower Garden" (below) was an experiment in using ten or fewer floral fabrics to create a watercolor effect; a technique the designer calls "Watercolor by Number." In this piece the two-inch squares are set on point, sashing separates the panels and appliqué finishes the scene.

ABOVE: "Watercolor Crucifix" *by Lucy A. Fazely, Oscoda, Michigan, 1998. 29 x 32 in.*
Photo by All American Crafts.

LEFT: "Ladybug's Flower Garden" *by Lucy A. Fazely, Oscoda, Michigan, 1996. 26 x 27 in.*
Photo by All American Crafts.

Appliqué

ABOVE & BACKGROUND:
"Exotic Petals" *by Marianna Kreider, Fort Wayne, Indiana, 2000. 88 x 108 in. Designed by Stitch 'N Chatter Quilt Club, Portland, Indiana.*
Photo by House of White Birches.

RIGHT & BELOW (DETAIL):
"Dragonfly Scroll" *by June Colburn Designs II, Largo, Florida, 1997. 21 x 47 in.*
Photo by J. Colburn.

The appliquéd, or "applied," quilt is the perfect showcase for the artistic freedom of the quilt maker. Although some designs have been passed down and used for hundreds of years, it is not essential to have a pattern for an appliqué quilt. The maker can take shapes from her world; the teapot on the stove, a leaf in the yard, her child's silhouette, and turn them into an appliqué shape to grace her next quilt. Lines are more flowing than patchwork, and the choices of subject and design are infinite.

Appliqué is much like painting. Appliqué designs can be as simple as one shape repeatedly stitched on a background fabric to very elaborate forms and panoramic scenes. The fabrics used and themes may have changed over the years, but many of the same techniques are still employed, though new technologies have brought quicker and easier methods, which have gained favor with many busy modern quilt makers.

Derived from the French word *appliquer*, appliqué means to apply. In the case of quilting, patches of one fabric are applied to a background fabric and secured with stitches. As with patchwork, the first use of appliqué will probably never be known. We do know that it was used in ancient Egypt and in the Middle Ages it was a cheap substitute for embroidery.

Again in this chapter you will find both antique and modern quilts, comparing how much quilts have changed while so many of the old traditions and techniques are still in use today.

Princess Feather

ABOVE: "Exotic Petals"
by Marianna Kreider, Fort
Wayne, Indiana, 2000.
88 x 108 in. Designed by
Stitch 'N Chatter Quilt Club,
Portland, Indiana.
Photo by House of White Birches.

BELOW: "Princess Feather,"
maker and date unknown.
90 x 92 in. In the collection
of Cindi Van Hurk.
Photo by Cheri Stearns.

From the mid-19th century, "Princess Feather" was a common pattern used throughout the United States. Named after the *fleur de lis* plume on the Prince of Wales' dress uniform, it was originally called "Prince's Feather." Green and/or red print appliqué on an off-white background was a standard coloration for this graceful and dynamic plumed design. The current owner of the quilt below purchased it from a dealer in the thumb area of Michigan, and it is presumed to be from that area.

This particular quilt is highly unusual in that each wheel has only six feathers, where eight is the norm with four sometimes being seen as well. Also unusual is the direction the plumes are turning. Typically the plumes turn in a clockwise direction, while here they are moving in a counter-clockwise direction.

Although the feathers in this quilt are all one shape, the design demands skill with a needle in order to make its narrow stems and feathered edges. Some quilts have only one shape, such as a simple leaf, repeated throughout the quilt top and these are the most basic form of appliqué. "Exotic Petals" (see top of this page and page 46) is a beautiful example of how simple shapes can create a stunning quilt top. This pattern uses only two templates, each a partial circle. The curved pieces are appliquéd to the edges of square blocks. When the blocks are set together it creates a chain that dances across the top vertically and horizontally.

Butterfly

Nature motifs have long been a favorite with quilters, and the butterfly block is no different. According to the *Encyclopedia of Pieced Quilt Patterns* the first documented pieced butterfly pattern is from *Needlecraft* in 1928. Before that the blocks were appliquéd as in this antique quilt, "Summer Butterflies" (below left). These butterflies are a very simple shape that would not be recognizable without the embroidered edges, antennae, and the lines separating the body sections and wings. A central section of blocks is set with bold yellow sashing strips surrounding them, followed by two rows of butterflies also set with the wide yellow strips.

The bold butterflies in "Butterfly Block of the Month" (below right) are a mix of appliquéd and pieced butterflies, creating an interesting array of the beauties that would make a collector's heart flutter. The bold orange used in the blocks and sashing really makes this quilt pop.

A graceful, three-dimensional dragonfly rests on a stalk of summer rice in the elegant piece on pages 46 and 47. It was made of hand-dyed cotton batik, printed cotton, drapery cotton, velveteen, and sheer iridescent fabrics with silk ribbon and buttons to embellish it. Appliqué was applied by hand and machine, embroidery was done by hand, and quilting by machine. June Colburn, who has spent a great deal of time in Japan, describes her work as, "A unique blend of traditional Asian design motifs with a contemporary color palette."

BELOW LEFT: "Summer Butterflies," *date and maker unknown. 85 x 93½ in.* Photo by House of White Birches.

BELOW: "Butterfly Block of the Month" *by multiple designers, 1990s.* Photo by House of White Birches.

Flowers

Flowers are blooming everywhere on quilts! Since early times flowers have been a symbol of spring and new beginnings. Surely colonial quilt makers felt a ray of sunshine while working on a bright flower block on a cold winter day.

"T-Tulips," above, uses a combination of rather simple shapes to create these budding beauties. The quilt maker didn't want to stop having fun, just because the blocks were done and so she pieced blade and tumbler shapes for an interesting border treatment.

From the same period "Morning Glory," to the right, employs similar calico colors for a true touch of spring. It is interesting that the quilt maker used a wide white sashing that matches the background of the appliqué blocks thereby creating an unusual effect with the green cornerstone squares floating between the flowers.

Marcia Knopp is a modern quilter whose work exemplifies the art of hand appliqué and hand quilting, in a time of mainly machine work. The award-winning quilt seen below was inspired by, "creatures that use and enjoy my garden much more than I." Appliqué was done by the needle turn method with freezer paper templates used on top. It has some embroidery outlining individual motifs and is hand quilted. Knopp says, "I enjoy the artistic outlet. Once I started I was hooked. Now I quilt all the time." Marcia completes a new masterpiece about every two years.

Dresden Plate

Some quilts have an incredible history that spans generations. The antique "Dresden Plate" quilt above was originally made in the 1930s by Laura Thomas. It was then passed down to her daughter, Ida Thomas Manning then to Ida's son, Gerald Manning, whose wife restored it. It is held in safekeeping by the Mannings until a time when it can be passed to their son, Brian Manning.

When Nancy Manning set out to do the restoration she consulted Pat Hubbel-Boucher, a well-respected Certified Quilt Appraiser. In Nancy's words the quilt was, "...absolutely used and worn beyond hope. Fabrics were rotting and there were some cigarette burn marks on it." Under Pat's guidance, Nancy salvaged all fabrics that could be saved, purchased a new background and started searching for vintage fabrics to replace the patches that were lost. Wanting to keep as much with the spirit of the original quilt, she had it quilted by an Amish quilter who followed the same quilting pattern as that used 65 years earlier by Laura Thomas.

The "Dresden Plate" pattern actually employs a combination of techniques; first the blades are pieced together, then the plate is appliquéd to a background fabric. There are a number of versions of this design, and it is interesting to note how the two quilts below and right, with 70 years between them, are so similar. The antique version uses blocks twice the size of the modern version, yet both use the same number of blades, with four pointed dividing pieces, and a squashed diamond in a circle of the plate center.

Broderie Perse and Trapunto

ABOVE & BELOW:
"Painted Ladies" by an
unknown maker, circa
1930–40. 47 x 72 in. with
a 17 in. ruffle on three sides.
In the collection of M'liss Rae
Hawley, Freeland,
Washington.
Photo by Michael Hawley.

Twenty outrageous flower ladies were painted on fabric in the fanciful quilt on this page. It is entirely hand quilted in flower motifs and probably dates to the 1930s or 1940s. Nothing is known of the quilt or its maker, other than that she had a whimsical sense of humor and she probably enjoyed life to its fullest. Some of the flowers represented include the tiger lily, daffodil, bluebell, chrysanthemum, daisy, and tulip. Although this is not an appliqué quilt, we couldn't resist including the "Painted Ladies!"

Broderie Perse, or Persian embroidery, as seen on both quilts to the right, is a technique of cutting a motif from a printed whole cloth and then appliquéing it to a background fabric or a pieced quilt top. Trapunto, the technique of adding extra stuffing to produce a raised surface on the quilt, came from Italy in the late 1700s. Quilt designer Janet Jones Worley says, "Broderie perse and trapunto are both quilting techniques that modern quilters fall in love with once they learn the fast and easy way both techniques can now be accomplished."

Traditionally Broderie Perse starts with a piece of cloth with a large print. Early quilt makers used glazed chintz prints and would often cut the same repeated design to lay on a new cloth background. By separating the motifs from the otherwise busy background of the chintz and arranging

them in interesting configurations, a whole new design was created. The new backgrounds were usually white cotton, letting the designs stand out in stark contrast.

Trapunto, or stuffed work, is done by adding a piece of loosely woven fabric to the quilt back and then quilting the two layers together without a batting. A small hole is made in the backing, by pulling apart threads without breaking them if possible. Then, with a bodkin, a small amount of batting is inserted into the space to be raised. The threads on the backing are then carefully realigned. Once the stuffed work is finished, the top is layered with its batting and backing and quilted over the same lines around the trapunto. By adding tight, close lines of stitching to the remainder of the quilt, the raised work really stands out.

Baltimore Album

True masterpieces of needlework are the "Baltimore Album" quilts from the mid-19th century, of which the quilt below is a beautiful example. The quilts can have up to forty blocks usually made by a group of friends and family members to commemorate a special event, place, or person. Many of the blocks were signed with messages and signatures, making them historical documents as well as works of art. The designs used in the appliqué often reflect Maryland's society of the time. Motifs of flowers, landmarks, cornucopias, animals, and baskets are some of the most commonly used in these quilts.

"This is My Story, This is My Song" on the right is a wonderful album quilt that incorporates blocks that are meaningful to the maker depicting important aspects of her life. The Texas State Seal (second row, second column) and Great Seal (second row, third column) blocks show her pride in her home state and love for the United States. Some of the blocks are based on designs by professional quilt designers Elly Sienkievicz, Nancy Pearson, and Pat Andreatta, while others are antique replicas. The designer says about some blocks patterned from antique designs, "(they) took on special meaning as they reminded me of my father's love of roses, my mother's love of teapots and flowers, my daughter's love of birds and singing,...and the heart blocks for the love of a dedicated husband." The original appliquéd border, known as the *Green Pepper Border* for the pepper shapes, ties all the different blocks together.

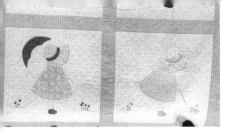

Sunbonnet Sue

"Sunbonnet Babies" were the creation of the artist Bertha Corbett Melcher. The babies, with their faces covered by large bonnets, were first published in 1902, the result of a friend's challenging comment that facial features must be shown in a drawing for a figure to show emotion. Melcher's babies became a great commercial success and eventually found their way onto dinnerware, postcards, and other goods.

"Sunbonnet Sue" (above and below) was made for Mary Lou Hummel when she was a small child by her aunt, grandmother, and great aunt. It is machine appliquéd and pieced, embellished with hand embroidery and finished with hand quilting. When researching the date the quilt was made Mary Lou looked in the diary of her uncle, Carroll Rice. Thinking they would mention the quilt on the day she was born, she looked under that day to find the only entry was about butchering a 500 pound hog. She was dismayed to find that her birth wasn't mentioned for another two weeks! The quilt, it turned out, wasn't made until she was five.

Within five years of Sunbonnet Sue's creation she was joined by her frequent companion, "Overall Bill" (below left). These motifs were popular as appliqué motifs in the 1930s. The figures were usually hand appliquéd and frequently embellished with embroidery.

Janet Jones Worley initially made a "Micro Mini Sue" (right) for her good friend, and fellow designer, Lucy Fazely. When Laurette Koserowski, editor of *The Quilter Magazine*, saw a picture of the incredibly small quilt she requested Janet make a sample for the magazine. Janet made two, which were then donated to the yearly auction by the Museum of the American Quilter's Society in Paducah, Kentucky.

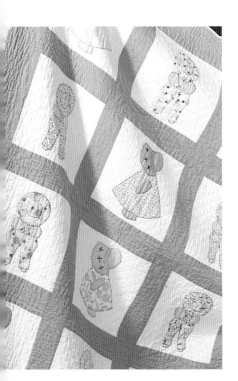

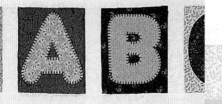

Other Techniques

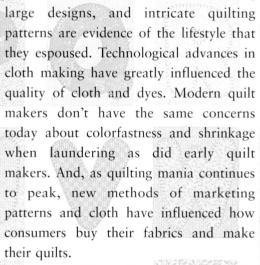

As we've seen, quilting has evolved over time. It is only natural to expect that with all our cultural diversity and innovations, that old techniques would evolve and new ones would be born. In this chapter we will look at some techniques that are not technically quilts, but rather bed covers. Nevertheless, because they are made of cloth and employ hand stitching techniques they are usually grouped in with quilts.

Quilting styles are very distinct to their makers; influenced by cultures, geography, religion, inherent skills, and the availability of supplies. The Hawaiians for example, never needed woven cloth for clothing or bed-covers. When they were introduced to quilting they developed their own unique style of whole-cloth appliqué. At the time, they didn't sew so they had no scraps and therefore never found the need to cut fabric into bits and patch them back together. Their quilts are like none in the world.

Another example can be seen in the quilts of the Amish, who were greatly influenced by their religion. Their choices of solid colored fabrics, large designs, and intricate quilting patterns are evidence of the lifestyle that they espoused. Technological advances in cloth making have greatly influenced the quality of cloth and dyes. Modern quilt makers don't have the same concerns today about colorfastness and shrinkage when laundering as did early quilt makers. And, as quilting mania continues to peak, new methods of marketing patterns and cloth have influenced how consumers buy their fabrics and make their quilts.

Where quilting will go from here is only speculation. Will the current resurgence of quilting remain high, or again lose favor for a period of time, only to resurface stronger than ever in years to come? Even during the low periods of interest, serious quilters will continue to ply their trade, in seclusion if necessary. This will assure that when the time is right, there will always be someone around to teach a new generation and the traditions will continue.

Cheater Cloth

ABOVE: "Handkerchief Quilt" *by Barbara MacDonald, Oscoda, Michigan, pieced in 1992, hand quilted in 1994.*
58 x 88 in.
Photo by Cheri Stearns.

RIGHT: "Lighthouse Memories" *by Carolyn Halt, Oscoda, Michigan, 1998.*
88½ x 88½ in.
Photo by All American Crafts.

BELOW: "Mother's Handkerchiefs" *by Noma Pfister, date unknown.*
68 x 81 in.
Photo by House of White Birches.

Cheater cloth is a piece of fabric with a quilt design printed on it. Quilters use the print as the complete quilt top, without having to do any patchwork or appliqué. The first cheater cloths were available in the mid-1800s and were imitation chintz patches. "Log Cabin" and "Charm" quilt prints became available in the early 1900s. The popular quilt designs of the 1930s, "Grandmother's Flower Garden," "Dresden Plate," and the "Double Wedding Ring," were offered by Sears. Cheater cloth is still printed today and modern quilters have a wide variety of choices to make doll quilts, baby quilts, and wall quilts, as well as bed quilts.

Although not a cheater cloth, the screen-printed panels in "Lighthouse Memories" (right) serve the same purpose. The 16 panels depicting Great Lakes lighthouses hold special memories for Carolyn Halt, the maker. She added a red strip and white corner to the bottom and right sides of each of the blocks and then set them with black sashing and red and white four-patch cornerstones just on the bottom and right sides. A wide black border was then added to the top and left sides of the quilt. The quilt was machine pieced and hand quilted.

Quilters are a resourceful lot that can, and will, make a quilt out of any woven fabric, no matter what the original purpose of it may have been. Men's neckties and ladies' handkerchiefs have often been made into quilts. Whether these quilts were made to use up materials at hand, to remember a special event, or as a memory quilt of a departed family member they are all unique in themselves.

Handkerchief quilts can be beautiful as well as a way to bring a person closer to their heritage. Barbara MacDonald says about the quilt at the top of the page that she made, "My father, Anthony Mucci, sent my mom, Lilly, a hanky from India during World War II that said 'Sweethearts, US Air Forces.' Many years later my mother asked if I could use it in a quilt. I collected hankies from my mom, mother-in-law and a couple from very dear friends. Plus, I still had a couple from when I was a little girl. The hankies are all sewn to each other, layered over muslin, batting and another layer of muslin. The entire quilt is hand quilted, with each hanky quilted differently."

Folded hankies can also be appliquéd in different shapes, as can be seen in the butterflies on the dainty quilt to the left.

Hawaiian and Amish

ABOVE & BELOW: "Woods & Waters" by Nancy Ehinger, West Branch, Michigan, 1976. 120 x 120 in.
Photo by N. Ehinger.

Hawaiian quilts are in a class by themselves. Hawaiians were first introduced to woven cloth and quilt making in 1820 when New England missionaries landed on their shores. The natives were not used to wearing clothing and up until then had no need to sew or weave their own cloth. Unlike the colonial women who used every scrap of fabric, the Hawaiians had no scraps and saw no need to cut up perfectly good cloth to make patchwork designs. Instead they used whole cloth, cut with a paper folding technique and, appliquéd it on to another whole cloth of the same size. The two cloths were in stark contrast to each other, often in bold colors such as red, orange, yellow, green, and blue. Not needing quilts for warmth in their tropical climate, the quilts were often sold or traded for other goods.

The appliqué designs were loosely based on their tropical surroundings, such as pineapples, leaves, seaweed, flowers, fruits, and palms, but rarely animals. Quilting was generally done in narrow bands that echo the outline of the appliqué, mimicking the waves in the ocean.

Although these overall appliqué designs are the most recognizable form of Hawaiian quilting, there are two other types of quilts that come from the islands. Quilts honoring the royal Hawaiian family were often made in red and gold or purple and gold, the royal colors, and used royal symbols in overall appliqué patterns. Flag quilts usually employed images of the English or American flags. Earlier, the Hawaiians had embraced the British flag as their own. When the islands came under the protection of the United States it was illegal to fly the British flag. Not wanting to lose their adopted flag, it was often incorporated into their quilts.

Just as the Hawaiians used their natural surroundings as inspiration, Nancy used the same techniques to design and make "Woods & Waters" (above and below), a Hawaiian style quilt. Living in Northern Michigan, she incorporated deer, evergreen trees, oak leaves, waves, and anchors into her appliqué design, depicting the forests and Great Lakes that surround the state.

Done in Christmas colors, this modern pillow (right) uses the anthurium in a Hawaiian style appliqué with the typical lines of echo quilting.

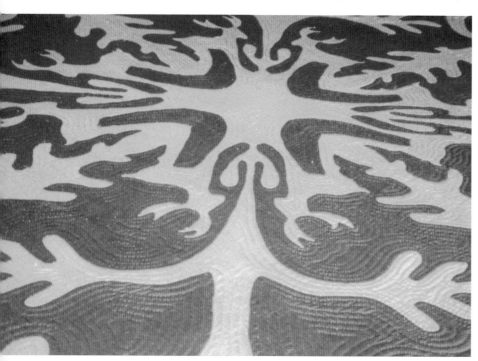

The Amish immigrated from Germany and Switzerland in the early 1700s and settled in Pennsylvania. They live strictly by the Bible and close to the land, shunning the outside world and its modern ways and technologies.

The Amish have taken the craft of quilt making and turned it into an art form of their own. They are known for their meticulous needlework and use of plain fabrics often set with black. Although they do use bright colors, the earth tones in the Amish style quilt to the right are typical, as is the "Roman Stripes" pattern. The Amish often piece large, simple yet striking quilt patterns. The plain fabrics and large pieces provide the perfect showcase for their close, fine, hand quilted stitches. The quilting designs are often elaborate, breaking from the constraints of simplicity in all other aspects of their lives. Heavily quilted bedcovers often have a combination of several quilting designs including feathers, scroll, cables, baskets, and wreaths.

ABOVE: "Amish Stripes" *by Barbara MacDonald, Oscoda, Michigan, 1995. 60 x 75 in. Machine pieced and hand quilted.*
Photo by Cheri Stearns.

LEFT: "Anthurium Wreath Pillow" *by Charlyne Stewart, Los Angeles, California, 1998. 18 x 18 in.*
Photo by House of White Birches.

Cathedral Window and Yo-yo

ABOVE (DETAIL) & BELOW:
"Yo-yo Quilt" *by Mrs. Rabitoy, circa 1970s. 61½ x 76 in. In collection of Doris Bonsole of Oscoda, Michigan.*
Photo by Cheri Stearns.

RIGHT: "Patched Cathedral Window" *by Patsy Moreland, 1998.*
Photo by House of White Birches.

According to *The American Heritage College Dictionary* the definition of a quilt is, "A coverlet or blanket made of two layers of fabric with a layer of cotton, wool, feathers, or down in between, all stitched firmly together." The techniques shown on these two pages are not really classified as quilts. They use fabric stitched together to make bedcovers, clothing, and decorative items, but that is where the similarities end. Even though they are not traditionally layered with a batting and backing, they often find themselves thrown in with quilts for the lack of a better place to put them. Both are traditionally pieced by hand, and since they start as small units they are a favorite of hand piecers to take with them wherever they go.

"Cathedral Window" is a design that starts with a square of fabric that is stitched and folded in a dizzying array of steps before being stitched to similar pieces. The steps are actually quite simple if you know what you are doing, but much too in-depth to describe here. Once the pieces are all joined, a decorative panel, such as the elongated nine-patch shown to the right, is placed on top and the edges of the folded square are brought around and tacked down to cover the raw edges of the panel.

The "Yo-yo Quilt," popular in the 1920s and 1930s, is an adaptation of the "English Suffolk Puff Quilt." It does not fall under the technical name of a quilt because it is generally one layer, not the usual three layers of quilt top, batting, and backing. The "Yo-yo Quilt" shown on this page is unusual in that it is tacked to a lining that is brought around in a wide binding, probably to stabilize it and preserve it. Each of the 1,872 little pieces started as a larger circle, in this case the template used is known to have been a coffee can. The edge is turned under a quarter of an inch to the wrong side of the fabric, then a running stitch is taken around the outside edge through the two layers. The thread is pulled tight, until the entire edge is gathered into a small circle. After the thread is tied off, the piece is flattened out with the gather centered on the top of the yo-yo. The small circles are then hand stitched to each other, forming the quilt top.

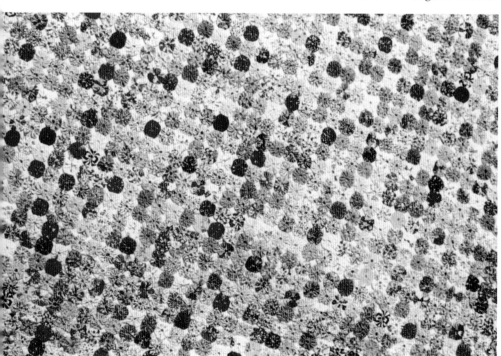

Reverse Appliqué

ABOVE (DETAIL) & BELOW RIGHT: Detail of "Mola," 15½ x 11½ in. square of a 68 x 34 in. quilt, circa 1960–80. In the collection of June Colburn.
Photo by J. Colburn.

BELOW: "Pair of Birds," circa 1960. 17½ x 14 in. In collection of June Colburn.
Photo by J. Colburn.

Reverse appliqué is done in a vastly different manner than regular appliqué. Traditional appliqué starts with a background and small pieces are applied to it. In reverse appliqué two to seven layers of fabric are cut away from the top and the raw edges sewn underneath, to reveal the fabrics below.

The Cuna Indians of the San Blas Islands, off the coast of Panama, have taken the technique and perfected it. In the 19th century, traders brought sewing supplies and cloth to the Indians. At the time they expressed themselves in body painting, which would eventually be replaced with the reverse appliqué designs they added to their clothing. The colors predominantly used are red, black, and orange, with just about any other color being used in smaller amounts. When a color is needed in only a small area of the design a small piece of cloth is inserted into the work, rather than using a whole layer of it.

All spaces are appliquéd on the *Mola*, as it is called—there are not any empty spaces. Designs are expanded to fill spaces and abstract designs are also used as filler. Design inspirations for *Molas* come from village and jungle life and can include birds, animals, plants, and sea life.

This *Mola* below left was purchased in Bogota, Columbia in 1974 for approximately $25. June Colburn, the current owner says it was "probably made in the 1960s." The *Mola* shows signs of wear, indicating that it had been worn (on a shirt) before it was sold. "The birds have their beaks touching, crests on their heads, and large triangular wings which fill the outside edges of the *Mola*. A stylized flower grows between the birds." June also notes, "One indication of its contemporary date is the use of hand embroidery for details on the birds' heads and necks."

LEFT: "Flower Garden Wall Hanging" by Karen Neary, Amherst, Nova Scotia, Canada, 1995. 38 x 48 in. Photo by House of White Birches.

The second *Mola* quilt in June's collection (left hand page top and bottom right) was purchased in Naples, Florida, in 1993 for $150. "The quality of the *Molas* varies from crude to exceptional, as in (this) square," June says.

Another group of Indians that has made a mark on quilting are the Seminole Indians of Florida. Originally from the Creek Nation in Georgia they were pushed south as the Europeans settled the Atlantic coast in the early 1700s. By the mid-18th century they were joined in the Gainesville area by other tribes and the name "Seminole" was used for the group, regardless of their differences. By 1860 most Indians had been forced from Florida, leaving just a few hundred hiding out in the Everglades. It was these hold outs that were responsible for the patchwork technique now called "Seminole Patchwork." This style of piecing was developed in conjunction with the use of a treadle sewing machine. The basic technique involves long strips of fabric, usually ripped not cut, stitched together and then cut apart and reassembled into geographic designs. The traditional colors used are red, yellow, green, and blue with white or black as a background.

"Flower Garden Wall Hanging" (above) is a modern quilt that uses Seminole piecing in several variations. Many of these same designs are being used in modern quilts, using the same technique; only it is now called "strip piecing."

Whole Cloth

Some of the earliest recorded quilts have been unpieced and unadorned by appliqué. Whole cloth quilting is the practice of putting two pieces of fabric together with a layer of batting between and then quilting a design, sometimes enhancing it with stuffed work or other fine handwork.

Fabric woven from linen and wool, "linsey-woolsey," was often used in early whole cloths quilts. This durable fabric was plentiful since flax was one of the more abundant crops in colonial America.

The white whole cloths seen on this page and commonly referred to as white-on-whites, can be machine quilted, but as these superior samples by Barbara MacDonald show, there is no better showcase for exquisite hand quilting stitches. Passionate quilters like hand quilting white-on-whites for the simple fact that they can get small, tight, even stitches consistently since there are no bulky seams to sew through.

Not all whole cloth quilts are white. Some fine examples have been on pastel, colored, or even all black fabrics. Print fabrics have been used, but the print hides the quilting designs, so solids are preferred. Because the entire design is based solely on the stitches, quilters enjoy being able to do heavily quilted designs that would be lost on a pieced quilt.

An outstanding example, "American White-on-White Quilt," (see page 79) was made by Rachel De Puy in 1805 showcasing her many talents with a needle. By combining several techniques she produced a beautiful and lasting testament to her creativity and artistic flair.

Some techniques commonly used with quilting on whole cloth quilts include embroidery, candlewicking, and trapunto. Corded quilting, a form of trapunto, is where two layers of fabric are stitched together with a running stitch in narrowly spaced parallel lines. From the back of the piece, cotton piping is then inserted and drawn between the stitching lines with a needle. These techniques give a whole cloth quilt a rich texture that cannot be achieved by quilting alone.

Block-a-Month

"Yikes" (right) is a new breed of quilt design called "Block-a-Month." The quilt pattern and the fabrics to complete the top are sold in monthly increments. This allows the modern quilt maker to purchase the pattern/fabrics for a small monthly fee instead of having to pay for the entire quilt at once. Today's busy quilt makers also like the idea that they have a schedule to follow, giving them one month to make each new block. "Block-a-Months" first came on the scene at the end of the 20th century and have grown into a big business. Debbie says of her design, "The name, 'Yikes,' expresses the sentiment everyone has when they first see it—it's very big and quite bright!" "Yikes" has easily been duplicated in many different fabric types and color schemes because its design lines are so bold and clean.

A designer who sells patterns internationally, Debbie says, "I often wonder what the archeologists will think when they discover ancient textiles that are identical, spread all over the globe; will they question just how much creativity our civilization had?"

"Deep Blue Sea" (below) is a very modern pictorial quilt that was set up as a "Block-a-Month" pattern. The quilt can be made all at once, or over the course of nine months, with each month's pattern and fabric purchased independently of each other.

Months of research went into this quilt, trying to achieve a realistic looking scene with the fish and other sea life as close to actual size as possible. Silhouettes of a whale, shark, squid, and barracuda give the piece a sense of depth. Princess Mirah Design Batik fabrics were selected to enhance the design. The rich colors and textures of the prints augment the designs and help bring them to life.

Machine appliqué, such as is used in this quilt, differs greatly from hand appliqué and is much faster to accomplish. A fusible web is pressed to the wrong side of the appliqué fabric. Then the pieces are cut out with no seam allowance added, the same size as they will appear on the quilt top. Once the appliqué pieces are arranged on the quilt top they are permanently fused with a hot steam iron. Raw edges are finished with a machine satin or buttonhole stitch. A stabilizer can be used under the piece to keep it from stretching as it passes through the sewing machine.

ABOVE: "Yikes" *by Debbie Bowles of Maple Island Quilts, Burnsville, Minnesota, 2000. 82 x 104 in.*
Photo by D. Bowles.

BELOW: "Deep Blue Sea" *by Lucy A. Fazely, Oscoda, Michigan. Machine quilted by Mary Ellen Sample of Florida and Michigan, 2000. 66 x 84 in.*
Photo by L. Fazely.

Stained-glass

ABOVE (DETAIL) & BELOW:
"Rose Arbor Stained Glass"
*by Nancy H. Ehinger, West
Branch, Michigan, 2001.
96 x 108 in. In collection of
Terry Boyce, West Branch,
Michigan.*
Photo by N. Ehinger.

Quilters have a long history of doing charitable works and being involved with community affairs. The lovely stained-glass quilt on this page was designed by Nancy Ehinger and made by the "Out To Lunch Bunch Quilters" in West Branch, Michigan. Their group has been meeting weekly for almost a quarter of a century. This quilt was then donated to Hospice of Helping Hands and raffled, with the proceeds going to the hospice program. The quilt was actually assembled in sections, and then those were joined together forming the complete quilt top. Nancy tells that it took three yards of black fabric to make the bias binding for the quilt's "leading."

Stained-glass quilts are similar to traditional appliqué in that the patches are cut out and applied to a background. In this technique the edges do not need to be turned under, just stitched down around the edges to hold it in place. A narrow black bias binding is then hand stitched over the appliqué edges to simulate the "leading." The binding must be cut on the bias, a 45 degree angle from the threads, for it to stretch along the sides of the appliqué creating smooth curves. These quilts can be as breathtaking as their glass counterparts.

Nancy's "Door Wall Stained-glass Quilt," above, was another quilt that was made by her group. "This quilt was made to quell the cold Michigan winter drafts coming through the door wall in our dining room. It can pulled up into the wooden cornice made by my husband, Del, by way of a series of pulley cords," Nancy says.

Modern quilters have of course found a way to make short work, even of this technique. Using a fusible web, the patches can be fused to the background. The bias binding can be stitched in place using a sewing machine's hemming stitch. Or, a bias tape is manufactured with a fusible web on the underside so that too can be fused in place, replacing tedious hours of stitching.

ABOVE: "Door Wall Stained Glass Quilt" *by Nancy H. Ehinger, West Branch, Michigan, 1992.*
84 x 100 in.
Photo by N. Ehinger.

Machine Appliqué

The whimsical quilt to the right was made as part of a quilt guild challenge called "Go for the Gold" to commemorate the Summer Olympic Games coming to Atlanta, Georgia, in 1996. A challenge was put to the Heritage Quilters of Huntsville, Alabama, to make a quilt with bright yellow fabric somehow related to the theme, although it did not have to be sports related. Diana Hofmann decided the gold would be a goldfish that got revenge on a hungry cat. She always uses a cat in her challenge quilts and didn't want this quilt to be an exception. This cat is heavily machine embroidered and covered with vinyl to simulate a bowl. The air bubbles are sewn-on acrylic rhinestones. The triumphant and smiling fish is made of orange/gold lamé.

Machine Appliqué is the stitching down of the appliqué edges with a buttonhole or satin stitch (a tight zigzag stitch). Machine embroidery uses a wide variety of stitches to embellish the quilt top and enhance the design. Most artists set their machines so they can move the fabric freely under the needle, creating the design stitch by stitch, using a free-motion technique. Hoops are made to be used with machines so the fabric can still be pulled taut, just as in hand embroidery. A wide variety of new threads in a rainbow of colors and metallic tones, used with special needles, give the modern thread artist an almost unlimited palette to work with.

Designer June Colburn draws on her time in Japan to create quilts with a distinct Japanese flavor. "Cranes" (above and below) was machine pieced from silk and vintage Japanese silk obi combined with embroidery from a vintage Japanese wedding kimono. The piece was finished with machine appliqué, embroidery, and quilting.

Redwork

ABOVE & BOTTOM:
"Redwork" by unknown maker, date unknown. 78 x 96 in. In the collection of Cindi Van Hurk.
Photo by Cheri Stearns.

BELOW: *"Redwork" by unknown maker, date unknown. 78 x 82 in. In collection of Cindi Van Hurk.*
Photo by Cheri Stearns.

"Redwork" is all the craze for present day quilters and it's easy to see why. The designs are delightful and recall a simpler life. The simple embroidery stitches are easy to make and since they are usually done in small blocks, the projects are portable.

A simple backstitch is one of the most common stitches in "Redwork," with the featherstitch, stem stitch, split stitch, and French knots also used. The floss is usually red or blue because, in the 1800s, Turkey red and indigo blue were both considered "safe," meaning the colors did not run or fade. More recently green and other colors have been used with the new colorfast dyes and flosses available.

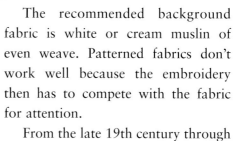

The recommended background fabric is white or cream muslin of even weave. Patterned fabrics don't work well because the embroidery then has to compete with the fabric for attention.

From the late 19th century through the 1930s penny squares were popular. These were muslin squares that had the designs marked on them and they sold for a penny each. Penny squares were, therefore, a predecessor to today's "Block-a-Month" quilts.

Once a seamstress had enough penny squares completed she could stitch them together into a quilt top like the one at the top of the page that uses a featherstitch over the seams.

Or a sashing could be added between the blocks as can be seen in the quilt above left, usually red to complement the embroidery.

In seven panels "Sunbonnet Sue," works her way through the week on page 61. In the early days of colonial America country, women had a certain day of the week set aside for each chore, such as mending, washing, and baking. On Sunday, Sue gets a well-needed day of rest!

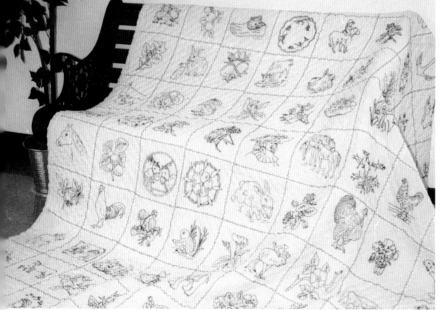

ABC Baby

In colonial days, learning to sew was a skill little girls learned early, sometimes as young as three or four years old. It was necessary for them to start young so they could have their baker's dozen of quilts made for their dowry before they wed. Often they would make samplers, learning new stitches with each design. Children were taught other skills early too, because it was a widely held belief that they were there to be functioning members of society. Although the modern ABC baby quilt below uses new techniques, a similar quilt made by a young colonial girl could have served as an English lesson as well. Reading and writing would have been a secondary lesson to the needlework.

BELOW: "ABC Baby Quilt" *by Cheryl Fall for Coats & Clark, 2000. 35 x 46 in.* Photo by House of White Birches.

Bibliography

American Heritage College Dictionary, The, Houghton Miflin Company, Boston, MA and New York, New York, 1993.

Bacon, Lenice Ingram: *American Patchwork Quilts,* William Morrow & Company, Inc., New York, New York, 1973.

Baird, Ljiljana: *Quilts,* Courage Books, Philladelphia, Pennsylvania, 1994.

Binney 3rd, Edwin, & Binney-Winslow, Gail, from the collection of: *Homage to Amanda,* Rutledge Hill Press, Nashville, Tennessee, 1984.

Bishop, Robert: *New Discoveries in American Quilts,* E. P. Dutton & Company Inc., New York, New York, 1975.

Brackman, Barbara: *Encyclopedia of Pieced Quilt Patterns,* American Quilter's Society, Paducah, Kentucky, 1993.

Fox, Sandi: *Small Endearments—Nineteenth-Century Quilts for Children and Dolls,* Rutledge Hill Press, Nashville, Tennessee, 1994.

House of White Birches: *Easy Nine-Patch Quilting,* Berne, Indiana, 1998. Edited by Sandra L. Hatch and Jeanne Stauffer.

House of White Birches: *Quick & Easy Scrap Quilting,* Berne, Indiana, 2000. Edited by Jeanne Stauffer and Sandra L. Hatch.

Ickis, Marguerite: *The Standard Book of Quilt Making and Collecting,* Dover Publications, Inc., New York, New York, 1949.

Johnson, Mary Elizabeth: *Mississippi Quilts,* University Press of Mississippi, Jackson, Mississippi, 2001.

Lang Graphics: *The 1998 American Quilt Calendar,* Lang Graphics, Delafield, Wisconsin, 1997.

Lewis, Alfred Allen: *The Mountain Artisans Quilting Book,* Macmillan Publishing Co., Inc., 1973.

Magaret, Pat Maixner & Donna Ingram Slusser: *Watercolor Quilts, That Patchwork Place,* Bothell, Washington, 1993.

McMorris, Penny: *Quilting,* a guide to accompany the television series produced by WBGU-TV, Bowling Green State University, 1981.

McMorris, Penny: *Quilting II,* a guide to accompany the television series produced by WBGU-TV, Bowling Green State University, 1982.

Newman, Thelma R.: *Quilting, Patchwork, Appliqué, and Trapunto,* Crown Publishers, Inc., New York, New York, 1974.

www.quilting.about.com

www.AmiSimms.com

RIGHT: "American White-on-White Quilt" *by Rachel De Puy, 1805.*
Photo by Peter Harholdt/CORBIS.

Further Resources

Quilt Patterns Etc.
Janet Jones Worley
Red Oak Road
Huntsville, AL
www.quiltpatternsetc.com

Mallery Press, LLC
Ami Simms
4206 Sheraton Drive
Flint, MI 48532-3557
Tel: 800-278-4824
www.AmiSimms.com

Maple Island Quilts
Debbie Bowles
www.mapleislandquilts.com

The Iosco County Historical Society Museum
405 West Bay Street
East Tawas, Michigan 48730

Museum of the American Quilter's Society
Paducah, Kentucky
www.quiltmuseum.org

All American Crafts, The Quilter Magazine
243 Newton-Sparta Road
Newton, New Jersey 07860
www.thequiltermag.com

House of White Birches
Quick & Easy Quilting, Quilt World
306 E. Parr Road
Berne, Indiana 46711
www.whitebirches.com

Lucy Fazely Designs
PO Box 492
Oscoda, MI 48750
www.lucyfazely.com

Little Foot, Inc., Lynn Graves
PO Box 1027
Chama, NM 87520
www.littlefoot.net

Index